BRILLIANT
BIRDS

Copyright © Marshall Editions 2016
Part of The Quarto Group
The Old Brewery, 6 Blundell Street,
London, N7 9BH

First published in the UK in 2016 by QED Publishing

A catalogue record for this book is available from the British Library.

Publisher: Maxime Boucknooghe
Editorial Director: Laura Knowles
Art Director: Susi Martin
Editorial development by Nancy Dickmann
Text by Matthew Morgan and Suhel Ahmed
Designer: Clare Barker
Production: Nikki Ingram

ISBN 978-1-78493-611-2

Originated in Hong Kong by Cypress Colours (HK) Ltd
Printed and bound in China
by 1010 Printing International Ltd

10 9 8 7 6 5 4 3 2 1   16 17 18 19 20

BRILLIANT
BIRDS

QED

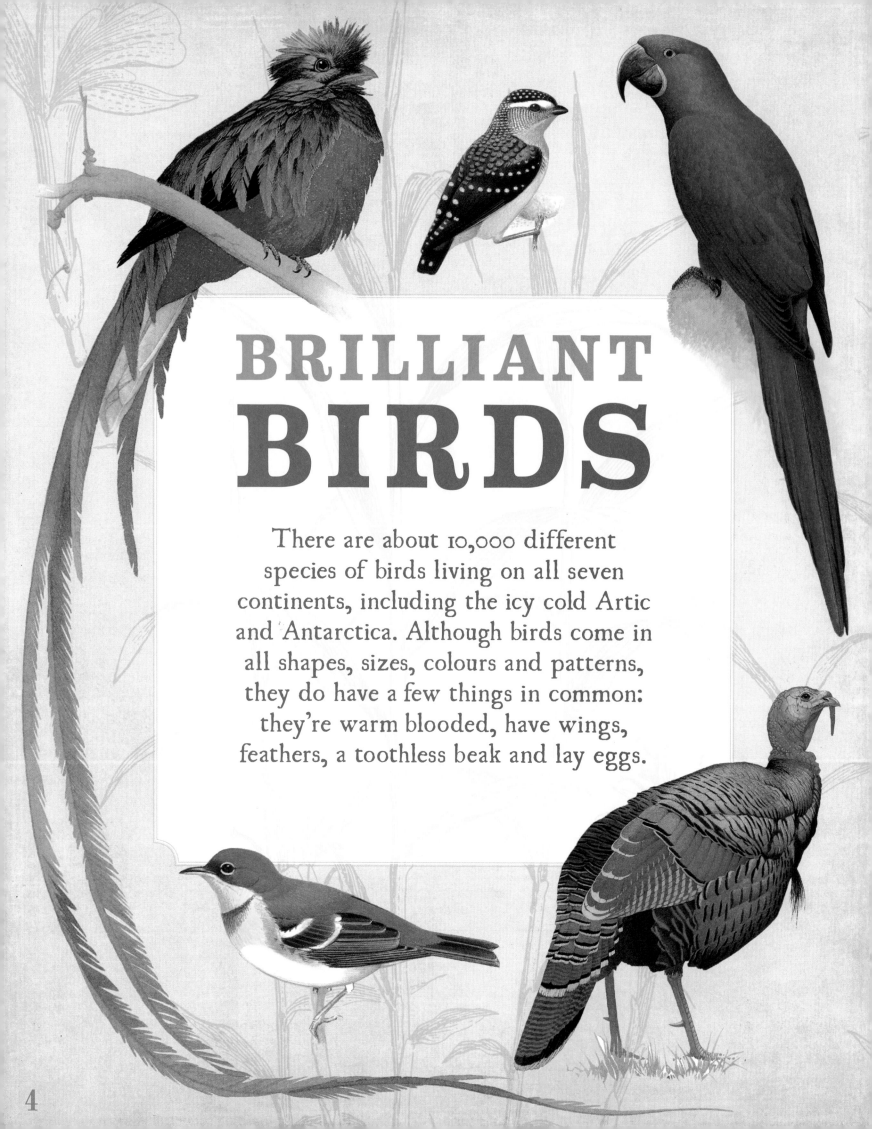

BRILLIANT BIRDS

There are about 10,000 different species of birds living on all seven continents, including the icy cold Artic and Antarctica. Although birds come in all shapes, sizes, colours and patterns, they do have a few things in common: they're warm blooded, have wings, feathers, a toothless beak and lay eggs.

In this beautifully illustrated guide
we've scouted the entire planet to bring
you some of the most impressive birds.
You'll meet birds of paradise of the
South Asian rainforests, prized for their
eye-catching feathers and plumage; the
marabou stork famed for the fleshy bit of
skin dangling from its throat. And then
you'll also discover birds like the glossy
ibis and whimbrel, with their amazingly
long beaks that are adapted to catch
food in rivers, lakes and seas.

Turn over to begin your world tour and
get ready to be dazzled by some of
the most vibrant and interesting
birdlife on Earth.

ATLANTIC PUFFIN
NORTH ATLANTIC AND
ARCTIC OCEANS
coast, oceanic

**CURL-CRESTED
ARACARI**
AMAZONIAN PERU, WEST
BRAZIL, NORTH BOLIVIA
tropical forest

GREAT WHITE PELICAN
SOUTHEASTERN EUROPE,
ASIA, AFRICA
inland lakes, marshes

The white pelican
can hold more than
50 mugs of of water
in its bill.

SHOEBILL
EAST CENTRAL AFRICA
marshes

TOCO TOUCAN
EASTERN SOUTH AMERICA
*tropical evergreen forest, tropical
grassland, farmland*

BLACK SKIMMER
USA; WINTERS IN
SOUTHERN USA, CENTRAL
AND SOUTH AMERICA
*coastal waters, rivers and
lakes with sandbanks*

GREAT HORNBILL
INDIA, SOUTHEAST ASIA
tropical evergreen forest

GREEN WOODHOOPOE
AFRICA, SOUTH OF
THE SAHARA
*woodland, mostly
near rivers*

UNBELIEVABLE BEAKS

A bird's beak is the bony, elongated
part of a bird's skull. Apart from using
it as an eating tool, birds also use their
beaks to groom feathers, communicate,
defend their territory and fend off
competitors.

WHITE-TIPPED SICKLEBILL
CENTRAL AND SOUTH
AMERICA
*subtropical or tropical
lowland or forest*

GREAT WHITE PELICAN
SOUTHEASTERN EUROPE,
ASIA AND AFRICA
*swamps and shallow
lakes*

RED-BILLED SCYTHEBILL
EASTERN PANAMA TO
NORTHERN ARGENTINA
swampy and humid forest, woodland

TAKAHE
NEW ZEALAND
(SOUTH ISLAND)
high valleys

KAKAPO
NEW ZEALAND
(SOUTH ISLAND)
mountain forest

FLIGHTLESS FANCIES

More than 40 living bird species do not have flying abilities. They range from the tiny (and strangely named) inaccessible island rail to the huge ostrich – the largest living bird in the world.

OSTRICH
AFRICA
savannah, semi-desert

EMU
AUSTRALIA
deciduous forest, desert

FLIGHTLESS
CORMORANT
GALAPAGOS ISLANDS
coastal waters

INACCESSIBLE ISLAND RAIL
INACCESSIBLE ISLAND (SOUTH ATLANTIC)
tussock grass

Which flightless bird
lives in Australia?

WEKA
NEW ZEALAND
scrubland

GALAPAGOS PENGUIN
GALAPAGOS ISLANDS
coastal waters

FABULOUS FEATHERS

Out of all the creatures on Earth today, only birds have feathers. As well as helping birds to fly, feathers keep them warm and waterproof. Birds also use feathers to communicate.

RAGGIANA BIRD OF PARADISE

SOUTHERN AND NORTHEASTERN NEW GUINEA
tropical forest

BLUE BIRD OF PARADISE

MOUNTAINS OF SOUTHEAST NEW GUINEA
rainforest

KING OF SAXONY'S BIRD OF PARADISE

MOUNTAINS OF NEW GUINEA
rainforest up to 2900 m

TUI

NEW ZEALAND AND COASTAL ISLANDS
forest, suburban areas

SUNBITTERN
SOUTHERN MEXICO TO
BOLIVIA AND BRAZIL
tropical forest

MANDARIN DUCK
EASTERN ASIA, CHINA, JAPAN,
INTRODUCED WORLDWIDE
fresh water

RUFFED GROUSE
ALASKA, CANADA
AND NORTHERN USA
*deciduous and conifer forest and
abandoned farmland*

The colour of flamingo
feathers can range from
shades of pink to a deep
crimson red.

GREATER
FLAMINGO
SOUTHERN EUROPE,
PARTS OF ASIA
AND AFRICA
fresh water, coast

NICOBAR PIGEON
ANDAMAN AND NICOBAR ISLANDS,
EAST OF PHILIPPINES
small, off-lying wooded islands

SNOWY OWL

ARCTIC TO NORTHERN
USA, EUROPE AND ASIA
*coast, tundra,
freshwater areas*

GOLDEN EAGLE

NORTH AMERICA, EUROPE,
NORTHERN ASIA AND AFRICA
*northern forest, high ground,
temperate grassland*

OSPREY

ALMOST WORLDWIDE
coasts, fresh water, farmland

PHILIPPINE EAGLE

PHILIPPINES
rainforest

TERRIFYING TALONS

Many birds of prey have developed
huge hooked claws with which
to stab and kill their prey. Without
them, most would not be able to
catch their food.

BLACK COLLARED HAWK

MEXICO TO PARAGUAY AND ARGENTINA
*tropical lowlands, open country
near water*

NORTHERN GOSHAWK

NORTH AMERICA, EUROPE,
NORTHERN ASIA
deciduous forest

Golden Eagles can
swoop down on their
prey at speeds of more
than 200 kph.

SNAIL KITE

FLORIDA (USA), CARIBBEAN,
MEXICO, CENTRAL AND
SOUTH AMERICA
freshwater marshes

**NORTHERN
EAGLE OWL**

NORTH AFRICA, EURASIA
(NOT BRITISH ISLES)
*wild countryside, hills with
tree cover and desert edge*

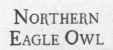

AMERICAN HARPY EAGLE

SOUTHERN MEXICO TO NORTHERN
ARGENTINA
lowland rainforest

DOUBLE-TOOTHED
BARBET

AFRICA
*tropical evergreen forest,
tropical grassland, farmland*

COCK-OF-THE-ROCK

NORTHERN
SOUTH AMERICA
tropical evergreen forest

GARNET PITTA

MALAYSIA; SUMATRA;
BORNEO
tropical evergreen forest

The northern cardinal
is the mascot of many
sports teams in the United
States. It is also the state
bird of seven US states.

PINE GROSBEAK

EUROPE, NORTHERN ASIA,
NORTH AMERICA
*northern and deciduous
forest, farmland*

NORTHERN
CARDINAL

NORTH AMERICA
*inhabited areas,
deciduous forest*

SCARLET TANAGER

EASTERN NORTH AMERICA
*deciduous forest,
northern forest*

RED-HEADED TROGON
NEPAL, SOUTH CHINA, SOUTHEAST ASIA
forest

RED AVADAVAT
INDIA, PAKISTAN, SOUTHWEST CHINA, SOUTHEAST ASIA
scrub, grassland, reedbeds, farmland

CRIMSON TOPAZ HUMMINGBIRD
NORTHERN SOUTH AMERICA
lowland rainforest

CARDINAL HONEYEATER
MELANESIAN ISLANDS (NOT NEW GUINEA)
tropical evergreen forest

RAVISHING IN RED

Some birds have bright red feathers. They use their fancy plumage to show off how fit and healthy they are to mates, and to intimidate competitors.

VERMILLION FLYCATCHER
SOUTHWEST NORTH AMERICA, CENTRAL AND SOUTH AMERICA
scrub, savanna, riparian woodland

COMMON TURKEY
USA, MEXICO
forests; brushland

PRAIRIE CHICKEN
CENTRAL USA
farmland; temperate grassland

Which wattled bird can be found on farmlands in the USA?

SOUTHERN GROUND-HORNBILL
PARTS OF AFRICA SOUTH OF THE EQUATOR
tropical grassland

BEARDED BELLBIRD
PARTS OF NORTHERN SOUTH AMERICA
forest and woodland

DOUBLE-WATTLED CASSOWARY
NEW GUINEA, NORTHERN AUSTRALIA
forest

WATTLES AND WOBBLY BITS

Many birds have strange, fleshy bits of skin called wattles hanging from their throats. Males often use them in their courtship displays. The bigger or more colourful the wattle, the more attractive he will appear to a mate.

MAGNIFICANT FRIGATEBIRD
CENTRAL AMERICA, SOUTH AMERICA
coastal waters; bays, islands, estuaries

THREE-WATTLED BELLBIRD
HONDURAS TO WESTERN PANAMA
tropical forest

MARABOU STORK
TROPICAL AND SUBTROPICAL AFRICA
large wetlands and open country

AMAZONIAN UMBRELLABIRD
NORTHERN SOUTH AMERICA
virgin forest, islands in larger rivers

AUSTRALIAN OWLET-NIGHTJAR

AUSTRALIA, TASMANIA, SOUTH NEW GUINEA
forest, woodland, scrub

SEE-SEE PARTRIDGE

SOUTHERN RUSSIA),
IRAN TO NORTHWEST INDIA
*arid foothills and
semi-desert*

CRAFTY CAMOUFLAGE

Although some brightly coloured birds like to stand out, there are other birds that have developed camouflage to protect themselves from predators.

GREY POTOO

WEST INDIES, CENTRAL
AND SOUTH AMERICA
*deciduous forest, tropical
evergreen forest*

GREAT TINAMOU

SOUTH AMERICA
*rainforest and lowland
evergreen forest*

SNOW GOOSE

ARCTIC NORTH AMERICA; WINTERS ON
MEXICAN COAST
*breeds on Arctic tundra; winters on
freshwater and salt marshes, farmland*

TAWNY FROGMOUTH
AUSTRALIA, TASMANIA
*forest, open woodland,
trees in scrub,
gardens, parks*

SNOW BUNTING
ARCTIC, NORTHERN EUROPE,
NORTHERN ASIA, NORTH AMERICA
*coast, tundra, high ground,
temperate grassland*

ROCK PTARMIGAN
ARCTIC AND NORTHERNMOST PARTS
OF EUROPE, ASIA, AND NORTH
AMERICA
tundra, high ground

Which well-camouflaged
bird is the star of a
famous Christmas carol?

COMMON QUAIL
EUROPE, PARTS OF ASIA, AFRICA; WINTERS
MEDITERRANEAN COAST, AFRICA, ASIA
grassland, farmland

COMMON PRATINCOLE
SOUTHERN EUROPE,
SOUTHWEST ASIA, AFRICA
*open land, sun-baked mud
flats, freshwater banks*

BROWN-BACKED
NEEDLETAIL
INDIA, SOUTHEAST ASIA
AND THE PHILIPPINES
forest up to 6,000 ft

NORTHERN GOSHAWK
NORTH AMERICA, EUROPE,
NORTHERN ASIA
deciduous forest

EUROPEAN ROLLER
BREEDS IN EUROPE, NORTH AFRICA,
SOUTHWEST ASIA. WINTERS IN EAST AND
SOUTH AFRICA, MIDDLE EAST
forest, woodland, open country

The northern goshawk is
an aggressive bird that is
likely to attack anything
that comes too close.

GYRFALCON
ARCTIC EUROPE, ASIA,
NORTH AMERICA,
GREENLAND, ICELAND
*mountains, tundra,
sea cliffs*

RUFOUS FANTAIL
LESSER SUNDA AND WEST
PAPUAN ISLANDS, AUSTRALIA,
COASTAL NEW GUINEA,
MELANESIA, MICRONESIA
forest, mangroves

PEREGRINE FALCON
WORLDWIDE, EXCEPT ANTARCTICA
*coast, temperate grassland, tundra,
high ground*

FANTASTIC FLYERS

Birds share the skies with
insects and bats, but no animal
is able to fly as far or as fast
as these impressive flyers.

WHITE-THROATED SWIFT
WESTERN USA, CENTRAL AMERICA
high ground, desert

EURASIAN HOBBY
BRITAIN TO CHINA; WINTERS IN AFRICA
AND FAR EAST
open country, bush, savanna

SPEED KINGS

Although some of these birds can fly and others can't, they can all move fast on the ground.

GREATER RHEA
SOUTH AMERICA
tropical grassland

CREAM-COLOURED COURSER
AFRICA, CANARY AND CAPE VERDE ISLANDS;
SOUTHWEST ASIA, WEST INDIA
desert and semidesert

CORNCRAKE
EUROPE, ASIA, AFRICA
grassland, farmland

RED-LEGGED SERIEMA
SOUTH AMERICA
tropical grassland

GREATER ROADRUNNER
SOUTHWESTERN USA, MEXICO
desert, scrub, grassland

The secretary bird is the only bird of prey that spends more time walking than in flight.

CASSOWARY
NEW GUINEA; AUSTRALIA
tropical evergreen forest

RUNNING COUA
SOUTHWEST MADAGASCAR
arid brush

SECRETARY BIRD
AFRICA, SOUTH OF THE SAHARA
tropical grassland

RED KITE
EUROPE, MIDDLE EAST,
NORTHERN AFRICA
*deciduous forest,
temperate grassland*

KEA
NEW ZEALAND (SOUTH ISLAND)
forest, open country

Which carrion eaters
from this selection do
not have curved beaks?

SNOWY SHEATHBILL
SUBANTARCTIC ISLANDS AND
SOUTHERN SOUTH AMERICA
WHEN NOT BREEDING
coasts

BEARDED VULTURE
SOUTHERN EUROPE, AFRICA,
MIDDLE EAST TO CENTRAL ASIA
mountains

AMERICAN CROW
SOUTHERN CANADA, USA
*open country, farmland,
open woodland, parks*

CRESTED CARACARA
SOUTHERN USA; CENTRAL AND SOUTH AMERICA
open country

TURKEY VULTURE

TEMPERATE AND TROPICAL
NORTH AND SOUTH AMERICA,
FALKLAND ISLANSDS
plains, desert, forest

CARRION EATERS

....

The dead and decaying carcass of an animal may not sound very appetising to us, but to these birds it is an essential source of food.

BATELEUR

AFRICA, SOUTH OF THE
SAHARA, SOUTHWEST ARABIA
savannah and plains

KING VULTURE

MEXICO, CENTRAL AND
SOUTH AMERICA
*tropical grassland,
tropical
evergreen forest*

LAPPET-FACED VULTURE

PARTS OF AFRICA, SAUDI
ARABIA, YEMEN, OMAN
*desert, high ground, tropical
grassland*

CITRINE CANARY FLYCATCHER

PHILIPPINES, GREATER
SUNDA ISLANDS
forest, woodland

SUN PARAKEET

SOUTH AMERICA: GUYANA,
SURINAM, FRENCH GUIANA,
NORTHEAST BRAZIL
open forest, savanna

GOLDEN-BACKED WOODPECKER

INDIA, SOUTHEAST ASIA TO
THE PHILIPPINES
woodland, forest fringe, mangroves

After saffron toucanet chicks hatch, both mother and father share the child-rearing duties.

YELLOW-THROATED LONGCLAW

AFRICA, SOUTH OF THE
SAHARA
tropical grassland, farmland, fresh water

NORTHERN PARULA

NORTH AND CENTRAL AMERICA,
WEST INDIES
deciduous forest, fresh water

BLOND-CRESTED WOODPECKER

SOUTH AMERICA
forest

ALLURING YELLOW

These brightly coloured birds are truly eye-catching. Spotting a yellow feather on the ground is considered lucky and is said to bring happiness.

SAFFRON TOUCANET
SOUTHEAST BRAZIL
rainforest

GREAT KISKADEE
SOUTHEAST TEXAS, CENTRAL AND SOUTH AMERICA
groves, orchards, wooded banks of streams

WHITE THROATED GERYGONE
SOUTHEAST NEW GUINEA, COASTAL AUSTRALIA
open forest, woodland

COMMON TODY-FLYCATCHER
SOUTHERN MEXICO, CENTRAL AND SOUTH AMERICA
open country, plantations, parkland

YELLOW-FOOTED GREEN PIGEON
INDIAN SUBCONTINENT
dense forest

GOLDEN ORIOLE
EUROPE, ASIA, NORTHWEST AFRICA
inhabited areas, deciduous forest, tropical evergreen forest

GLOSSY IBIS
CENTRAL AMERICA, AFRICA, EUROPE, ASIA, AUSTRALASIA
coast, fresh water

EURASIAN OYSTER CATCHER
EUROPE, COASTAL AFRICA, COASTAL ASIA NORTH OF THE EQUATOR
farmland, coast, coastal water

LONG-BILLED SPIDERHUNTER
MALAYSIA, SUMATRA, BORNEO
moist, dense forest

LONG BEAKS

Some birds have extremely long beaks to help them find and catch food more easily.

WHIMBREL
WORLDWIDE, EXCEPT POLAR REGIONS AND SOUTHERN EUROPE
breeds on moors, tundra; winters on shores, estuaries, marshes

SWORD-BILLED HUMMINGBIRD
SOUTH AMERICA
high ground (above 2100m)

AMERICAN WOODCOCK

NORTH AMERICA, EAST
OF THE ROCKIES
temperate forest, farmland

The average sword-billed hummingbird is around 10 centimetres long, with a beak that can be longer than its body!

HOOPOE

EUROPE, ASIA, AFRICA
*inhabited areas, farmland,
grassland, deciduous and
tropical forest*

RUFOUS-TAILED JACAMAR

MEXICO, CENTRAL AND
SOUTH AMERICA
*tropical evergreen forest,
fresh water*

LONG-BILLED WOODCREEPER

NORTHERN SOUTH AMERICA
tropical evergreen forest

BROWN KIWI

NEW ZEALAND (NORTH ISLAND)
deciduous forest

MALLEEFOWL
SOUTH AUSTRALIA
mallee scrub (arid eucalyptus woodland)

WILD TURKEY
USA, MEXICO
forest, field, orchard, marsh

GREAT BUSTARD
SOUTHERN AND CENTRAL EUROPE, ASIA
farmland, temperate grassland

At nearly 20 kilograms, the great bustard is the heaviest flying bird in the world.

MUTE SWAN
TEMPERATE EURASIA, NORTH AMERICA, SOUTH AFRICA AND AUSTRALIA
lowland freshwater lakes and marshes, coastal lagoons and estuaries

SHOEBILL
EAST CENTRAL AFRICA
marshes

VICTORIA CROWNED PIGEON

INDONESIA NEW GUINEA, BTAK AND YAPON ISLANDS
coast, fresh water, tropical evergreen forest

EMPEROR PENGUIN

ANTARCTIC COASTS
ocean and pack ice

WESTERN CAPERCAILLEE

NORTHERN EUROPE
deciduous forest, northern forest

BIG AND HEAVY

Not all birds are delicate and light. Some birds have grown larger so they can survive in their habitats and defend themselves against predators.

CALIFORNIA CONDOR

USA: CALIFORNIA
mountains

GUANAY CORMORANT
PERU AND CHILE
coastal habitats

AMAZING NESTS
·········

Birds use their nests as a place to lay eggs and raise their young. Nests can vary enormously, from intricately woven basket-like shelters to holes in the ground.

EDIBLE-NEST SWIFTLET
ANDAMAN AND NICOBAR ISLANDS, SOUTHEAST ASIA, PHILIPPINES
coasts, islands; feeds over forests and scrub

BURROWING OWL
SOUTHWEST CANADA, WESTERN USA, FLORIDA, CENTRAL AND SOUTH AMERICA
grassland, deserts, sparse farmlands, airports, golf courses

AFRICAN PALM SWIFT
AFRICA, SOUTH OF THE SAHARA
open country

LONG-TAILED TAILORBIRD
INDIA, SOUTHEAST ASIA, SOUTH CHINA
thickets, scrub, bamboo, gardens

CAHOW

BREEDS ON EASTERN BERMUDA
*open seas; breeds on
five rocky islets*

**BLACK-BROWED
ALBATROSS**

SOUTHERN OCEANS
open ocean

Which of these birds
makes its home by
digging a hole in
the ground?

CRESTED TREE SWIFT

INDIA, SOUTHEAST ASIA
open woods, clearings, gardens

MONK PARAKEET

SOUTH AMERICA AND
NORTHEAST USA

*open woodland, palm groves, cultivated
land, eucalyptus plantations*

ABBOTT'S BOOBY

EASTERN INDIAN OCEAN
open sea

RED-FOOTED BOOBY
ALL TROPICAL OCEANS
open sea

MOTTLED PETREL
SOUTH AND NORTH PACIFIC
oceanic

GREAT CORMORANT
EVERY CONTINENT EXCEPT
ANTARCTICA AND SOUTH AMERICA
coast, fresh water

Brown pelicans dive
into the water and scoop
fish and water into their
pouch. They then rise to
the surface, drain
the water and swallow
the catch.

MACARONI PENGUIN
SUBANTARCTIC, SOUTH
AMERICA
oceanic; breeds on coasts

COMMON KINGFISHER
EUROPE, NORTH AFRICA TO ASIA,
INDONESIA, NEW GUINEA AND
SOLOMON ISLANDS
*inland waterways, marshes,
mangroves, sea shores*

NORTHERN GANNET
NORTH ATLANTIC OCEAN
coast, coastal waters

COMMON TERN
NORTH AMERICA, EUROPE, COASTAL
AREAS IN THE SOUTHERN HEMISPHERE
coast, fresh water

DIVING CHAMPIONS

·····················

These birds have become
experts at plunging into
water to catch fish or
other food.

BROWN PELICAN
PACIFIC COAST (CALIFORNIA
TO CHILE), WARM WESTERN
ATLANTIC WATERS
coast, coastal waters

RED-THROATED DIVER
NORTH AMERICA, NORTHERN
ASIA, NORTHERN EUROPE
*fresh water, tundra,
coastal water*

AMERICAN
BLACK VULTURE

EURASIAN
CUCKOO
*(from a Meadow
Pipit nest)*

At 1.5 kilograms, the
ostrich egg is the largest
egg of any living bird.
The bee hummingbird
lays the smallest bird
egg, which weighs only
half a gram.

OSPREY

BEE
HUMMINGBIRD

BRONZE-WINGED
COURSER

BLACK-NECKED
GREBE

MEADOW
PIPIT

PEREGRINE FALCON

OSTRICH

AFRICAN JACANA

STRIPE-BACKED
BITTERN

BARN OWL

EURASIAN
CUCKOO
*(from a Great Reed
Warbler nest)*

GREAT
REED
WARBLER

GREY PLOVER

WINDING CISTICOLA

EXCELLENT
EGGS

······················

All birds lays eggs.
The size of the egg and the
patterns, markings and
colour of the shell vary
according to species
and breed.

LESSER BIRD
OF PARADISE

BLACK CROW

WINDING
CISTICOLA

GREYISH SALTATOR

CHILEAN TINAMOU

WHITE-THROATED
LAUGHING-THRUSH

WINDING
CISTICOLA

BLUE BIRD

RESPLENDENT QUETZAL
MEXICO, CENTRAL AMERICA
*tropical evergreen forest,
high ground*

LESSER GREEN BROADBILL
MALAYSIA, SUMATRA, BORNEO
forest on lowland and hills

GREEN AND GORGEOUS

Most of these beautiful
green-feathered birds are
from the tropics.

SPECTACLED PARROTLET
CENTRAL AND SOUTH AMERICA
open forest, thorn bush

AFRICAN EMERALD CUCKOO
AFRICA, SOUTH OF THE SAHARA
forest edge and clearings

SUPERB FRUIT DOVE
AREAS OF THE PHILIPPINES, INDONESIA AND NORTHEAST AUSTRALIA
*forest, forest edge, river banks,
cultivated land with trees*

RED-TUFTED MALACHITE SUNBIRD
AFRICA
high ground, tropical grassland

BLUE-CROWNED MOTMOT
MEXICO, CENTRAL AND SOUTH AMERICA
farmland, tropical evergreen forest

EMERALD TOUCANET
SOUTH MEXICO TO NICARAGUA, VENEZUELA, COLOMBIA, ECUADOR AND PERU
humid mountain forest, open country with tree

The quetzal is the national bird of Guatemala and also appears on the country's flag. The nation's currency is named after the bird, too.

LONG-TAILED SYLPH HUMMINGBIRD
VENEZUELA TO BOLIVIA, PERU AND ECUADOR
forest, scrub

GOLDEN-TAILED WOODPECKER
AFRICA, SOUTH OF THE SAHARA
woodland, brush, mountain forest

CRIMSON BREASTED BARBET
PAKISTAN EAST TO CHINA AND PHILIPPINES, SOUTH TO SRI LANKA, SOUTHEAST ASIA, SUMATRA, JAVA, AND BALI
woodland, gardens, urban areas

ANHINGA
SOUTHERN USA TO ARGENTINA
lakes, rivers

SCARLET IBIS
VENEZUELA, COLOMBIA,
COASTAL GUIANAS AND
BRAZIL, TRINIDAD
*coastal swamps,
mangroves, lagoons,
estuaries, mudflats*

GREAT EGRET
WORLDWIDE EXCEPT COLD
NORTHERLY PLACES
fresh water, coastal water

LOVELY AND LONG

Long-legged birds such as
ibis, egrets and cranes live on
or near water, where their
long limbs help them wade in
search of prey.

RED-LEGGED SERIEMA
SOUTH AMERICA
tropical grassland

BLACK WINGED STILT

EURASIA AND AFRICA: TROPICAL,
SUBTROPICAL AND TEMPERATE LATITUDES
*mainly freshwater swamps, marshes,
lagoons*

AMERICAN BITTERN

CENTRAL NORTH AMERICA; WINTERS
IN SOUTHERN USA, CARIBBEAN,
MEXICO, CENTRAL AMERICA
*fresh and saltwater marshes,
swamps and bogs*

Which bird, whose loud
call can be heard over
several kilometres, is not
only the tallest bird in
North America but also
among the rarest?

REDSHANK

EUROPE, ASIA,
NORTHERN AFRICA
*farmland, grassland,
fresh water,
coastal water*

COMMON CRANE

EUROPE, ASIA
*farmland, temperate
grassland, fresh water*

WHOOPING CRANE

NORTHERN CANADA,
SOUTHERN USA
*temperate grassland, fresh
water, coastal water*

SECRETARY BIRD
SUB-SAHARAN ARFICA
open grasslands and savannah

AFRICAN FINFOOT
AFRICA, SOUTH OF THE SAHARA
wooded streams, pools, mangroves

YELLOW-THROATED LONGCLAW
AFRICA, SOUTH OF THE SAHARA
tropical grassland, farmland, fresh water

The Northern Jacana's large toes allow it walk across floating plants in lake and fresh-water marsh habitats.

LITTLE GREBE
EUROPE, ASIA, NEW GUINEA AND AFRICA
freshwater lakes and coastal waters

AFRICAN HARRIER HAWK
AFRICA, SOUTH OF THE SAHARA
forest, savanna, open grassland

NORTHERN JACANA
CENTRAL AMERICA,
WEST INDIES
fresh water

BLACK BUSTARD
SOUTH AFRICA
semi-arid scrub and dunes

FUNNY FEET
....

Most birds walk on their toes
rather than their entire feet.
This can result in some
extremely long toes, which
help distribute the bird's
weight over a wide area.

GOLDEN-TAILED
WOODPECKER
AFRICA
*tropical forest and
grassland*

COMMON MOORHEN
WORLDWIDE (NOT AUSTRALASIA)
*swamps, marshes, ponds, slow
rivers with cover on banks*

CRESTED SERPENT
EAGLE
INDIA TO SOUTH CHINA,
SOUTHEAST ASIA, INDONESIA,
PHILIPPINES
forest

FIERCE
HUNTERS

Birds of prey, or raptors, are
meat-eating birds that use their
strong feet, talons and hooked
beaks to catch and kill prey.

BALD EAGLE
NORTH AMERICA
coasts, rivers and lakes

BELTED KINGFISHER
CANADA, UNITED STATES,
MEXICO, CENTRAL
AMERICA, AND THE
WEST INDIES
*near inland bodies
of waters or coasts*

RED TAILED HAWK
NORTH AND CENTRAL AMERICA,
WEST INDIES
*deciduous and tropical evergreen
forest, desert, farmland*

COMMON KESTREL

EUROPE, ASIA, AFRICA
AND THE EAST COAST OF
NORTH AMERICA
*fields, heaths, shrubland
and marshland*

RED-BACKED SHRIKE

EUROPE AND WESTERN ASIA
AND TROPICAL AFRICA
moorland and grassland

GYRFALCON

ARCTIC EUROPE, ASIA,
NORTH AMERICA,
GREENLAND, ICELAND
*mountains, tundra,
sea cliffs*

Which bird includes among
its prey not just snakes but
other reptiles, amphibians
and small birds?

PEL'S FISHING OWL

SUB-SAHARAN AFRICA
*forests along rivers
and lakes*

RUBY THROATED HUMMINGBIRD
BREEDS EASTERN NORTH AMERICA;
WINTERS SOUTHEASTERN USA TO
NORTHWEST COSTA RICA
woodland and swamp

BEE HUMMINGBIRD
CUBA AND ISLE OF PINES
*forest and forest edge, gardens;
occasionally in fairly open country*

LONG TAILED HERMIT
EASTERN MEXICO TO BOLIVIA
AND CENTRAL BRAZIL
*lowland forest understory and
tall secondary growth*

The baya weaver bird
often builds its nest so
that it dangles over water,
making it difficult for
predators to attack.

RUFOUS HORNERO
EASTERN SOUTH AMERICA FROM
BRAZIL TO ARGENTINA
groves of trees, open country

VILLAGE WEAVER
SUDAN AND ETHIOPIA
SOUTH TO ANGOLA,
CAPE PROVINCE
*forest, cultivated
land, gardens*

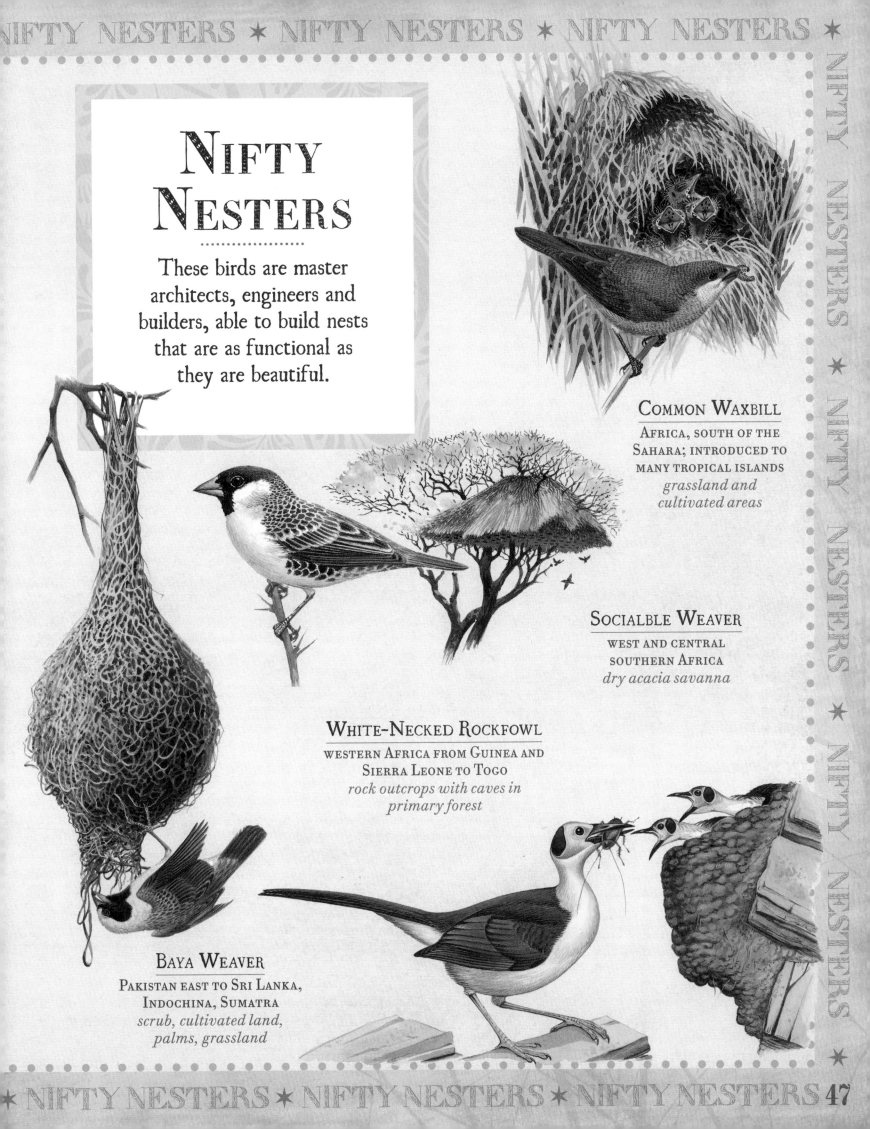

NIFTY NESTERS

These birds are master architects, engineers and builders, able to build nests that are as functional as they are beautiful.

COMMON WAXBILL

AFRICA, SOUTH OF THE SAHARA; INTRODUCED TO MANY TROPICAL ISLANDS
grassland and cultivated areas

SOCIALBLE WEAVER

WEST AND CENTRAL SOUTHERN AFRICA
dry acacia savanna

WHITE-NECKED ROCKFOWL

WESTERN AFRICA FROM GUINEA AND SIERRA LEONE TO TOGO
rock outcrops with caves in primary forest

BAYA WEAVER

PAKISTAN EAST TO SRI LANKA, INDOCHINA, SUMATRA
scrub, cultivated land, palms, grassland

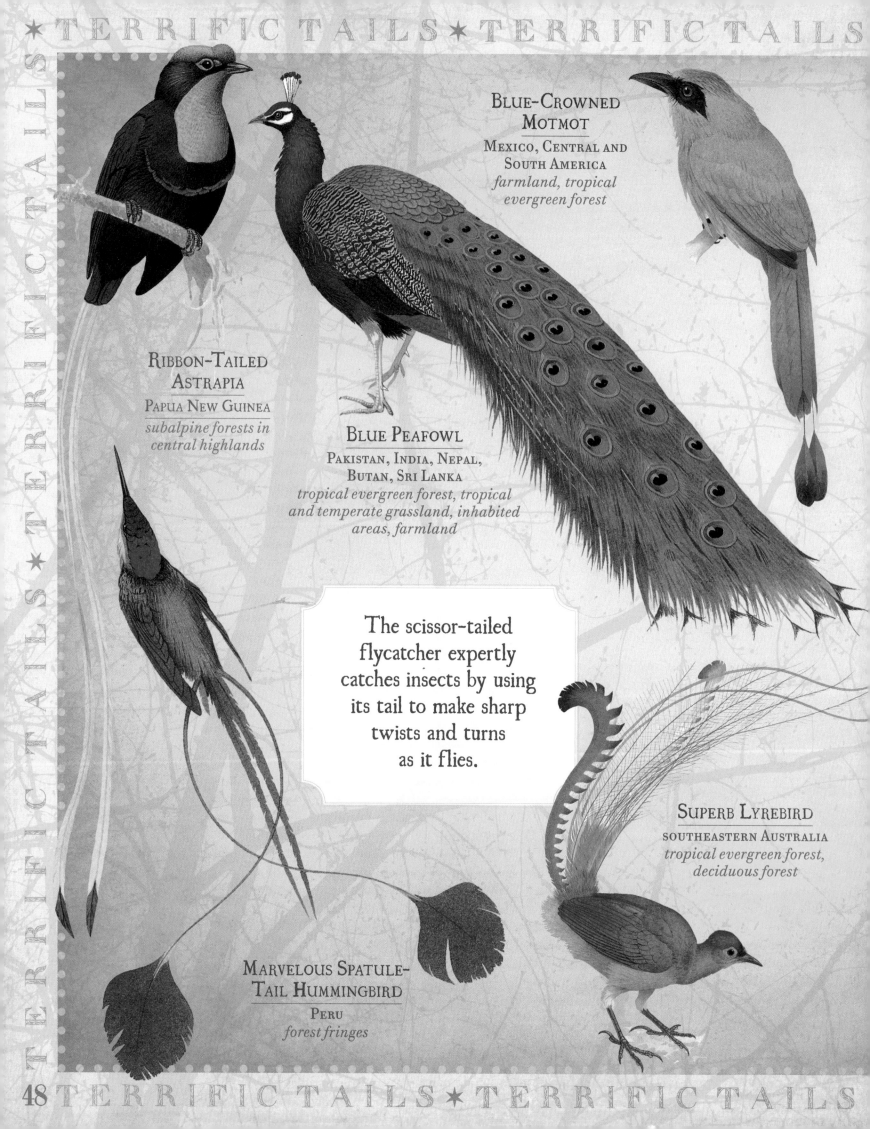

BLUE-CROWNED
MOTMOT
MEXICO, CENTRAL AND
SOUTH AMERICA
*farmland, tropical
evergreen forest*

RIBBON-TAILED
ASTRAPIA
PAPUA NEW GUINEA
*subalpine forests in
central highlands*

BLUE PEAFOWL
PAKISTAN, INDIA, NEPAL,
BUTAN, SRI LANKA
*tropical evergreen forest, tropical
and temperate grassland, inhabited
areas, farmland*

The scissor-tailed
flycatcher expertly
catches insects by using
its tail to make sharp
twists and turns
as it flies.

SUPERB LYREBIRD
SOUTHEASTERN AUSTRALIA
*tropical evergreen forest,
deciduous forest*

MARVELOUS SPATULE-
TAIL HUMMINGBIRD
PERU
forest fringes

RED-TAILED TROPIC BIRD
INDIAN AND PACIFIC OCEANS
coast, oceanic

GREATER RACQUET-TAILED DRONGO
PARTS OF ASIA
forest, cultivated land

PARADISE WHYDAH
EASTERN AND SOUTHERN AFRICA:
SUDAN TO ANGOLA; SOUTH
AFRICA: NATAL
dry open country

TERRIFIC TAILS

It is thought that birds with super-long tails use the feature mainly for courtship and display; in other words, to show off how attractive they are to potential mates, so they are chosen over competitors.

GOLDEN PHEASANT
WEST CHINA; INTRODUCED IN BRITAIN
scrub on rocky hillsides; introduced in woodland

SCISSOR-TAILED FLYCATCHER
SOUTHCENTRAL USA;
WINTERS SOUTHERN TEXAS,
MEXICO TO PANAMA
open grassland (prairie), ranchland

SPANGLED COTNGA
SOUTH AMERICA
forest, woodland, savanna

HYACINTH MACAW
CENTRAL BRAZIL, EASTERN
BOLIVIA, NORTHEAST
PARAGUAY
*dry forest along
watercourses, wet forest
edges, among palms*

BLUE BEAUTIES

Unlike pink and yellow
feathers, blue feathers are not
made from the food the bird
eats. It is the structure of the
feather itself, which affects
the way light falls on it, that
gives the feather its colour.

BLUE-BACKED MANAKIN
NORTHERN SOUTH AMERICA TO
SOUTHEAST BRAZIL, NORTH
BOLIVIA, TOBAGO
rain forest, secondary growth

**WATTLED FALSE
SUNBIRD**
EASTERN MADAGASCAR
forest

PURPLE HONEYCREEPER
TRINIDAD, SOUTH AMERICA
farmland, tropical evergreen forest

BLACK-NAPPED MONARCH

INDIA, SOUTHERN CHINA, SOUTHEAST ASIA TO LESSER SUNDA ISLANDS AND PHILIPPINES

forest, scrub, bamboo, cultivated land

BLUE DACNIS

CENTRAL AMERICA, TROPICAL SOUTH AMERICA

open forest, secondary growth, orange groves

SATIN BOWERBIRD

EASTERN AUSTRALIA

deciduous forest, tropical evergreen forest

The blue jay's fondness for acorns is partly why oak trees were able to spread after the last ice age.

COMMON PARADISE KINGFISHER

NEW GUINEA TO MOLUCCA ISLANDS

forest

ASIAN FAIRY BLUEBIRD

INDIA TO SOUTHEAST ASIA, GREATER SUNDA AND ANDAMAN ISLANDS, PHILIPPINES: PALAWAN

hill forest to 5600 ft

EASTERN BLUEBIRD

NORTH AMERICA, EAST OF THE ROCKIES AND INTO CENTRAL AMERICA

inhabited areas, farmland, deciduous and tropical evergreen forest

SUPERB FAIRYWREN

AUSTRALIA: VICTORIA TO QUEENSLAND; TASMANIA

woodland, savanna, parks

GOLDCREST

AZORES, NORTHERN
EUROPE AND
EASTERN ASIA
*conifer woods to 4500m,
also some broad-leaved
woods*

CALLIOPE HUMMINGBIRD

BREEDS IN WESTERN NORTH AMERICA.
WINTERS IN SOUTHWEST MEXICO
*mountain meadows, edges of
coniferous forest*

Which bird found in
Cuba is the smallest in
the world?

WHITE-BARRED PICULET

SOUTH AMERICA: GUYANA TO
NORTHERN ARGENTINA
forest, woodland, parks

RED-BREASTED PYGMY
PARROT

BURU, CERAM, NEW GUINA,
BISMARCK ARCHIPELAGO,
SOLOMON ISLANDS
mountain forest

ELF OWL

SOUTHEAST USA, MEXICO
*wooded canyons, deserts with
saguaro cactus*

PURPLE THROATED SUNBIRD

SOUTHERN ASIA, MALAYSIA,
INDONESIA, PHILIPPINES
*scrub, second growth forest,
mangroves, gardens*

RIFLEMAN
NEW ZEALAND AND
NEIGHBOURING ISLANDS
*forest and modified forest
habitats*

RUBY-THROATED
HUMMINGBIRD
CENTRAL AND NOTH AMERICA
deciduous and pine forest

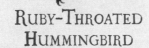

SHORT-TAILED
PYGMY TYRANT
NORTHERN SOUTH AMERICA,
EAST OF THE ANDES,
AMAZONIAN BRAZIL; PERU,
BOLIVIA, TRINIDAD
*high open rain forest,
clearings in forest,
plantations*

POCKET
SIZED

Some say that small is
beautiful, which must make
these tiny birds some of the
most beautiful in the world.

WINTER WREN
NORTH AMERICA, EUROPE,
NORTHERN AFRICA, ASIA
inhabited areas, deciduous forest

BEE HUMMINGBIRD
CUBA AND ISLE OF PINES
*forest and forest edge, gardens;
occasionally in fairly open country*

EUROPEAN ROBIN
EUROPE, NORTHERN
AFRICA, ASIA
inhabited areas, deciduous forest

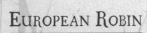

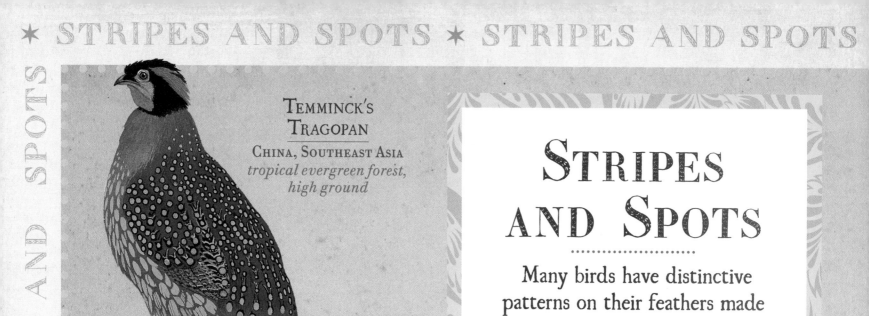

TEMMINCK'S TRAGOPAN
CHINA, SOUTHEAST ASIA
tropical evergreen forest, high ground

STRIPES AND SPOTS

Many birds have distinctive patterns on their feathers made up of spots and stripes. Often birds use these features to recognise members of their own species.

COMMON PHEASANT

EAST ASIA, CHINA, KOREA, JAPAN AND MYANMAR; INTRODUCED IN EUROPE, NORTH AMERICA, NEW ZEALAND
woodland, forest edge, marches, agricultural land

HELMETED GUINEAFOWL

EAST AFRICA
forest, dry brush

WHITE-FACED WHISTLING DUCK

TROPICAL SOUTH AMERICA, AFRICA, MADAGASCAR
lakes, swamps, marshes

OCELLATED ANTBIRD
TROPICAL NICARAGUA TO
PANAMA, SOUTHERN
COLOMBIA, NORTHWEST
ECUADOR
*undergrowth of humid,
lowland forest*

BARRED ANTSHRIKE
TROPICAL MEXICO, CENTRAL
AND SOUTH AMERICA
*varied, forest, brush, savanna,
gardens; rarely above 6600 ft*

RED-THROATED DIVER
NORTH AMERICA, NORTHERN
ASIA, NORTHERN EUROPE
*fresh water, tundra,
coastal water*

ZEBRA FINCH
AUSTRALIA, INDONESIA
*deciduous forest, temperate
grassland, farmland*

SPOTTED PARDALOTE
AUSTRALIA, TASMANIA
forest, woodland

Which of these birds
is named after another
well-known stripy animal?

GREY PEACOCK-PHEASANT
HIMALAYAS TO HAINAN; SOUTHEAST ASIA
forest

STARLING
EUROPE, ASIA; INTRODUCED
ALMOST WORLDWIDE
*inhabited areas, farmland, temperate
grassland, deciduous forest, tropical
evergreen forest*

RAINBOW LORIKEET
INDONESIA, NEW GUINEA, AUSTRALIA
*inhabited areas, farmland, deciduous and
tropical evergreen forest*

Cockatiels are often
ranked the favourite pet
bird. As well as being
affectionate and sociable,
they are relatively easy
and cheap to keep.

COCKATIEL
AUSTRALIA
open county

BLACK-CAPPED LORY
LOWLAND NEW GUINEA AND OFFSHORE ISLANDS
undisturbed rain forest, swamp forest

ROSE-RINGED PARAKEET

CENTRAL AFRICA, INDIA,
SRI LANKA; INTRODUCED IN
MAURITIUS, MIDDLE EAST,
SINGAPORE, HONG KONG,
HAWAIIAN ISLANDS
woodland, cultivated land

PERFECT PETS

....

There are many types of
pet birds, from parrots to
budgerigars, and each has its
own unique personality.

GREY PARROT

CENTRAL AFRICA:
WEST COAST TO KENYA AND
NORTHWEST TANZANIA
*lowland forest, savanna,
mangroves*

BUDGERIGAR

AUSTRALIA;
INTRODUCED INTO USA
*farmland, desert, forest,
grassland, scrub*

ROSY-FACED LOVEBIRD

SOUTHWEST AFRICA: ANGOLA,
NAMIBIA, SOUTH AFRICA
dry open country

GREAT CURASSOW

MEXICO TO ECUADOR
tropical evergreen forest

PILEATED WOODPECKER

NORTH AMERICA, MEXICO
deciduous forest

CRESTED TREESWIFT

SOUTHEAST ASIA
tropical evergreen forest

COOL CRESTS

As with many prominent features on birds, crests are generally used for display purposes.

LONG-EARED OWL

NORTH AMERICA, EUROPE,
NORTHWEST AFRICA, ASIA
farmland, deciduous forest

SULPUR-CRESTED COCKATOO

AUSTRALIA, NEW ZEALAND,
NEW GUINEA, INDONESIA, PALAU
tropical evergreen forest, tropical grassland, farmland

GREAT CRESTED GREBE
EUROPE, ASIA, AFRICA,
AUSTRALIA, NEW ZEALAND
fresh water

ROYAL FLYCATCHER
CENTRAL AND
SOUTH AMERICA
tropical evergreen forest

Which of these birds
is a popular but
demanding pet?

HOATZIN
SOUTH AMERICA: AMAZON
AND ORINOCO BASINS
tropical evergreen forest

LAPWING
EUROPE, ASIA, WESTERN AND
NORTHERN AFRICA
*farmland, temperate grassland,
fresh water*

**RED-BRESTED
MERGANSER**
NORTHERN EURASIA AND
NORTH AMERICA; WINTERS IN
MEDITERRANEAN, EAST CHINA,
GULF OF MEXICO
*breeds by rivers, estuaries
and coasts; winters on
estuaries and coastal bays*

BLACK CROWNED CRANE
AFRICA, SOUTH OF THE SAHARA
swamps

LONG-LEGGED BUZZARD
CENTRAL AND SOUTHEASTERN
EUROPE, EAST TO CENTRAL ASIA,
NORTH AFRICA
*mainly lowland, open country,
often arid or semi-arid*

WANDERING ALBATROSS
SOUTHERN OCEANS
coast, oceanic

SOARING SENSATIONS

These birds are some of the
most accomplished flyers in
the bird kingdom, and
include the bird with the
largest wingspan – the
wandering albatross.

BATELEUR
AFRICA, SOUTH OF
THE SAHARA,
SOUTHWEST ARABIA
*savanna and
plains*

BLACK STORM
PETREL
NORTHEAST PACIFIC OCEAN,
CALIFORNIA TO PERU
coastal and offshore waters

MANX SHEARWATER

ATLANTIC AND
PACIFIC OCEANS,
MEDITERRANEAN SEA
oceanic and coastal

SOUTHERN GIANT PETREL

SOUTHERN OCEANS. BREEDS ON
VARIOUS ISLANDS AND ON
ANTARCTIC COASTS
oceanic

Wandering albatrosses
can travel an impressive
16,000 kilometres
in a single journey.

PINTADO PETREL

ANTARCTICA AND THE
SUBANTARCTIC ISLANDS
oceanic

CALIFORNIAN CONDOR

NORTH AMERICA
*rocky shrubland, coniferous
forests, and oak savannas*

RAINBOW NATION

With a range of colours that would make a painter envious, these beautiful birds are not likely to go unnoticed by mates and competitors.

ECLECTUS PARROT
NEW GUINEA, NORTHEAST AUSTRALIA
tropical evergreen forest

SCARLET MACAW
MEXICO, CENTRAL AMERICA, NORTHERN SOUTH AMERICA
tropical evergreen forest

MANY-COLOURED RUSH-TYRANT
SOUTH AMERICA: PERU, SOUTHEAST BRAZIL, PARAGUAY, URUGUAY, ARGENTINA, CHILE
fields, meadows near water, swampy ground

MANDARIN DUCK
EASTERN ASIA, CHINA, JAPAN, INTRODUCED WORLDWIDE
fresh water

RED JUNGLEFOWL
SOUTHEAST ASIA
farmland, deciduous forest, desert

INDIAN PITTA

NORTHERN AND CENTRAL INDIA;
WINTERS IN SOUTH INDIA AND
SRI LANKA
*varied, including semi-cultivated
land and forest*

YELLOW CROWNED AMAZON

MEXICO, CENTRAL AMERICA,
PARTS OF SOUTH AMERICA
forest, wide range of wooded habitats

The Crimson Sunbird
feeds mainly on nectar
from flowers.

CRIMSON SUNBIRD

SOUTHEAST ASIA
*tropical evergreen forest, tropical
grassland, farmland*

EUROPEAN BEE-EATER

BREEDS IN EUROPE, SOUTH RUSSIA, NORTH
AFRICA, SOUTHWEST ASIA; WINTERS IN
TROPICAL AFRICA AND MIDDLE EAST
open country, woodland

RED-CRESTED TURACO

ANGOLA
tropical evergreen forest

CURL-CRESTED ARACARI

AMAZONIAN PERU, WEST BRAZIL,
NORTH BOLIVIA
forest

ANSWERS

FLIGHTLESS FANCIES

The Emu is a flightless bird from Australia. After the ostrich, it's the second largest bird in the world.

LOVELY AND LONG

The Whooping Crane is the tallest bird in North America. They can be up to 1.5 metres tall.

WATTLES AND WOBBLY BITS

The Prairie Chicken is found on farmland in the USA. It is becoming endangered as its prairie habitat is lost.

FIERCE HUNTERS

The Crested Serpent Eagle catches snakes and other reptiles, as well as amphibians and birds.

CRAFTY CAMOFLAUGE

The Partridge: in The Twelve Days of Christmas, "a partridge in a pear tree" is the last line of each verse.

POCKET SIZED

The Bee Hummingbird is the smallest, measuring 57 millimetres in length and weighing just 1.6 grams.

CARRION EATERS

The American Crow and Snowy Sheathbill have straight beaks.

STRIPES AND SPOTS

The Zebra Finch is named after the zebra because of its distinctive black and white stripes.

AMAZING NESTS

The Burrowing Owl nests in the old burrows of animals such as prairie dogs, or digs its own hole if the soil is soft and there are no burrows.

COOL CRESTS

The Sulphur-crested Cockatoo can be fun but demanding: it likes lots of attention and can be noisy.